Contents

Meet...

Sam   Dad   Mom

Sam the Cook

by Katrina Davino • illustrated by Katarina Gasko

Lucy Calkins and Michael Rae-Grant, Series Editors

LETTER-SOUND CORRESPONDENCES

m, t, a, n, s, ss, p, i, d, g, o, c, k, ck, r, u, h, b, e, f, ff, l, ll, j, w, y

HIGH-FREQUENCY WORDS

is, like, see, the, no, so, as, has, his, too, says, go, to, for, look, he, you

Sam the Cook
Author: Katrina Davino
Series Editors: Lucy Calkins and Michael Rae-Grant

Heinemann
145 Maplewood Avenue, Suite 300
Portsmouth, NH 03801
www.heinemann.com

Cataloging-in-Publication data is on file with the Library of Congress.

ISBN-13: 978-0-325-13822-0

Design and Production: Dinardo Design LLC, Carole Berg, and Rebecca Anderson

Editors: Anna Cockerille and Jennifer McKenna

Illustrations: Katarina Gasko

Photographs: p. 32 (empanadas) © hlphoto/Shutterstock; p. 32 (dumplings) © Absurdvirus/Shutterstock.

Manufacturing: Gerard Clancy

Printed in the United States of America on acid-free paper
3 4 5 6 7 8 9 10 MP 28 27 26 25 24 23
January 2023 printing / PO# 4500866727

Sam and Dad Cook

Dad likes to cook,

and Sam likes to cook too.

Sam asks,

"Did you cook pierogies as a kid?"

"Yes," Dad says.

Sam hops up so he can help.

He props up his doll,

so it can help too.

Sam dips a cup in the bag.

He dumps it in.

Sam pats the pierogies flat
and cuts them.

Dad fills up the pierogies.

Dad and Sam tuck in the ends.

The pierogies go in the pot.

"Yum! Did you cook pierogies?"
asks Mom.
"Yes!" says Sam.

Mom and Dad and Sam

dig in...

…and Sam's doll digs in too!

2

Yum! Hot Dogs!

Dad has the grill on,

so he can cook hot dogs.

Sam hands the hot dogs to Dad.

Jon and Kat get the buns.

Mom fills up the cups.

Em has a big sip and...ack!

Em has a big spill!

Yuck! Sam's bun is wet.

Dad looks at the bun.

It is so wet it drips. Yuck!

Dad pops the bun on the grill.

The bun gets hot and crisp.

Yum! Hot dogs!

Sam Cooks for Mom

The sun is not up yet.

But Dad is up,

and Sam is up too.

Sam looks in.

He sees yams, ham, and dill.

No, no, and no.

Sam looks and looks.

He sees eggs, milk, and plums.

Yes, yes, and yes!

The gas is on.

Dad melts the fat in the pan.

Sam drops it in,
and Dad flips it.

Dad cuts up a plum.

Sam adds mint on top.

Will Mom like it?

Yes!

31

DUMPLINGS

Pierogies, xiao long bao, samosas, ravioli, fufu, and empanadas. What do all these delicious foods have in common? They're all dumplings.

empanadas

Dumplings come from all over the world. *Fufu* is a sticky dumpling that comes from Ghana. You eat fufu with your fingers, and you dip it in a tasty stew. Yum!

An *empanada* is an extra crispy dumpling. In Chile, there's a famous kind of empanada called an *empanada de pino*. It's filled with ground beef, onions, hard-boiled egg, olives, and raisins. So many people in Chile love empanadas de pino!

xiao long bao

Xiao long bao come from China, and they're sometimes called "soup dumplings" because they're filled with hot soup. Be careful when you take a bite—the soup might spill out!

Ask your reader some questions like...

- What happened in this book?
- What are some steps that Sam and his dad did when they were making pierogies?

- How did Sam's hot dog bun get wet?
- Sam likes to cook. Have you ever tried cooking? Would you like to?